GROVER'S BOOK OF CUTE LITTLE WORDS

By Michaela Muntean
Illustrated by Carol Nicklaus

A SESAME STREET/READER'S DIGEST KIDS BOOK

Published by Reader's Digest Young Families, Inc.,
in cooperation with Children's Television Workshop

ISBN: 0-89577-710-X

Hello, everybody! It is I, lovable, furry old Grover, and I am here to tell you about words.

The words I am going to show you are not just any words. They are very cute, very little words. Right now, I am on my way to find my favorite little words. Would you like to come along?

A face is a good place to find little words, and here comes a face now!

Excuse me, sir, may I borrow your face for a minute?

This is an **ear**. Look at how cute the little word ear is. You will need to use your ears to hear all the other cute little words I am going to tell you.

This is a **nose**. Nose is a little word, but this is not a little nose. This face has a big nose.

Now look at the word **eye**. It is like a little letter sandwich made of two e's and a y in the middle. A face has two eyes and a nose in the middle!

Good-bye, sir, and thank you so much for letting us borrow your face!

EYE

NOSE

EAR

Everywhere I look I can see cute little words you would like to hear. Look up and see the **sky**.

Look down and see your **toes**!

FEET

PARK

My cute little toes are part of my **feet**. I can use my feet to walk to the **park**.

Look at my friends in the park! They are using their feet to run and jump and skip and play.

Oh, look! I see a **bee**! This small bee is near a tall **tree**. I know that there are three words in this tree that you would like to see. So come along, and follow me!

TREE

BEE

I cannot fly like that **bird**. I, Grover, will have to climb up this tree.

That bird has a **nest** in this tree.

Inside the nest, there are two blue **eggs**.

BIRD

EGGS

NEST

This tree was a good place to find cute little words.
Now I will climb down the tree to see what other things
we can find.

BUG

Oh, my goodness! There is a **bug**! The word bug is a very little word, and this bug is a very cute bug.

Oh, hello, Barkley! You are a very big **dog**, but dog is a very little word.

DOG

On the street, I see more things that have cute little word names. There is a red **car**, and a big yellow **bus**.

I see a **goat** in a **coat** getting on the bus. He is carrying a **box**. Let us ask him what is inside the box.

GOAT

COAT

Excuse me, Mr. Goat, but could we please see what is inside your box?

Oh, what a surprise! It is a **boat**. Did you know that goat, coat, and boat rhyme? You are taking a word family onto this bus! Congratulations, Mr. Goat!

BOAT

BOX

Here are two more families. One is a family of very cute **cats**. The other is a family of very little words.

One cat is sleeping on a **mat**.

One cat is wearing a **hat**.

One cat is holding a **bat**.

CAT

HAT

BAT

MAT

Oh, dear, the cat with the bat sat on the cat's hat. Now that cat has a flat hat, and he does not look happy.

I will give that cute cat a pat on the head and help him fix his hat.

Oh, this is such an exciting day! Everywhere we go, there are cute little words waiting for us. This **toy** store is a terrific place to find things that have cute little word names.

I see a **ball**, and a **doll**, and a **kite**. Cute little words are so much fun.

DOLL

KITE

BALL

BOOK

BAG

UP ↑

Now let us go **up** the stairs and see if there are any other things with cute little word names. We do not want to miss anything!

I was right again! Look at these books! Here is a **book** about cute little baby animals.

DOWN ⬇

I tell the clerk that I, Grover, would like to buy this book. The clerk puts the book in a **bag**.

I take the bag and walk **down** the stairs. There are so many things you can do with cute little words. It is amazing!

I can hardly wait to get home and show my mommy my new book!

I will run as fast as I can until I see my house.

I will put this cute little **key** into the keyhole. It will open the **door** to my house. Do you know who is behind this door?

DOOR

KEY

My **mommy**! Mommy is one of my favorite words. My mommy gives me a big hug. I tell her all about the cute little words we found today.

MOMMY

BED

Looking for little words makes me very tired. That makes me think of the cute little word **bed**.

I snuggle under my warm, snuggy blanket, and my mommy reads my new book to me.

There are only two more cute little words I want to tell you.
Look out my window at the night sky. Do you see that
shining **star**? Do you see the big full **moon**?
WHEW! Now I am ready to go to sleep.
Good night.

MOON

STAR